D1539534

# STEM IN CURRENT EVENTS

▸ Agriculture ▸ Energy ▸ Entertainment Industry ▾ **Environment & Sustainability**
▸ Forensics ▸ Information Technology ▸ Medicine and Health Care
▸ Space Science ▸ Transportation ▸ War and the Military

# ENVIRONMENT & SUSTAINABILITY

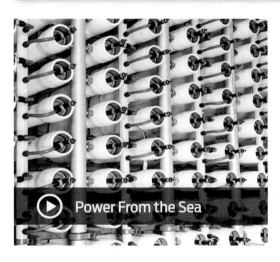

Power From the Sea

Growing Smarter Crops

Computer Technology in Weather Saves Lives

Agriculture

Energy

Entertainment Industry

Environment & Sustainability

Forensics

Information Technology

Medicine and Health Care

Space Science

Transportation

War and the Military

# STEM IN CURRENT EVENTS

# ENVIRONMENT & SUSTAINABILITY

By Michael Centore

MASON CREST

**Mason Crest**
450 Parkway Drive, Suite D
Broomall, PA 19008
www.masoncrest.com

Printed and bound in the United States of America.

First printing
9 8 7 6 5 4 3 2 1

Series ISBN: 978-1-4222-3587-4
ISBN: 978-1-4222-3591-1
ebook ISBN: 978-1-4222-8292-2

Produced by Shoreline Publishing Group
*Designer:* Tom Carling, Carling Design Inc.
*Production:* Sandy Gordon
www.shorelinepublishing.com

Front cover: Dreamstime: Asafta tl; Anke van Wyk tr. IDRISI b.

Library of Congress Cataloging-in-Publication Data on file with the publisher.

# Contents

## Key Icons to Look For

 **Words to Understand:** These words with their easy-to-understand definitions will increase the reader's understanding of the text, while building vocabulary skills.

 **Sidebars:** This boxed material within the main text allows readers to build knowledge, gain insights, explore possibilities, and broaden their perspectives by weaving together additional information to provide realistic and holistic perspectives.

 **Educational Videos**: Readers can view videos by scanning our QR codes, providing them with additional educational content to supplement the text. Examples include news coverage, moments in history, speeches, iconic sports moments, and much more!

 **Text-Dependent Questions:** These questions send the reader back to the text for more careful attention to the evidence presented here.

 **Research Projects:** Readers are pointed toward areas of further inquiry connected to each chapter. Suggestions are provided for projects that encourage deeper research and analysis.

 **Series Glossary of Key Terms:** This back-of-the-book glossary contains terminology used throughout this series. Words found here increase the reader's ability to read and comprehend higher-level books and articles in this field.

# INTRODUCTION
# Our Challenge

**H**umanity today faces many environmental challenges. Climate change, pollution, the limits of fossil fuels and other natural resources, overpopulation, food shortages, excessive carbon emissions…the list goes on. The threats these issues pose to our species and the world at large can be daunting to think about, much less find solutions for. Yet if we are to ensure the health of the planet for future generations, we have no other choice.

Environmental scientists are on the front lines of this battle. They may study forests, mountains, animals, oceans, weather patterns, or any of the whole host of things and processes that make up our natural surroundings. But no matter their focus, they all have one thing in common: discovering ways to protect our environment. Through their work and research, they show us that we are not separate from nature, but rather a part of it, and that we must learn to treat it as an extension of ourselves.

The field of environmental science uses all the elements of STEM: "hard sciences" such as chemistry, geology, and biology to examine the physical world and make connections between its elements; technological advances in computer science, digital mapping, genetics, and other areas; engineering principles to build better, more efficient ways of generating, storing, and reusing energy; and all sorts of math—from advanced algebra to geometry to statistics—to tie experimental data together and quantify changes in the environment.

Throughout this book, we'll see how environmental scientists are employing these and other principles to improve our understanding of the world. We'll follow soil scientists as they use synchrotron technology—like an X-ray, but for tiny particles—to test the effects of different fertilizers, and watch other scientists use genetics to create new breeds of trees that resist disease. We'll check out cutting-edge experiments with "clean fuels" and alternative energy sources. We'll examine how ecologists and landscape designers are working together to create spaces like the very cool "rain gardens" that are beginning to populate urban areas.

Our investigations aren't just limited to North America. We'll find out how Japanese environmental scientists are pioneering the use of "solar islands"—

*See this beautiful meadow? If we want to see the same scene in 100 years, we've got work to do right now.*

large floating assemblages of solar panels that provide lots of clean energy. We'll also get a look at a digital camera designed by Swedish researchers that can actually photograph the amount of methane (one of the key greenhouse gases) in the air, and see ways that solar power is improving sanitation facilities in India and Africa.

A little closer to home—in fact, in your own home—you'll see how you can participate in evolving environmental science technologies by using online tools like carbon calculators. These accessible, easy-to-use programs can help you stay informed about how much carbon trees in your area are taking out of the environment.

You'll also find out ways you can check your city or town's Air Quality Index, which measures the levels of pollutants in the air, and how to analyze your findings.

Such participatory moments are key to the future of environmental science and the well-being of our Earth. In addition to showing you some ways that scientists are reforming our relationship to the planet, this book will hopefully inspire you to incorporate their lessons into your day-to-day life. Scientific advances can move us forward. But unless people get involved, inform themselves, and try to change their habits for the better, they will only take us so far. Onward!

*Life begins in the dirt for this flower. A cutaway view shows the surprisingly complex root system that draws water and nutrients from the soil up into the plant.*

# SCIENCE AND
# Environment and Sustainability

## Words to Understand

**blight**   a widespread disease affecting plants

**decontaminate**   to remove dangerous substances from an area

**employ**   to make use of something

**infectious**   something that spreads rapidly

**infiltration**   in soil science, the process of water as it seeps into soil

**organic**   in agriculture, used to describe farming practices that do not involve pesticides and other man-made chemicals

The simplest place to look for environmental science at work is right under your feet: the soil itself, a mixture of decaying matter, air, water, nutrients, and living organisms. Soil is the outermost layer of the Earth and a crucial element of our survival. Without it, plants that provide food and give us oxygen would not be able to grow. It recycles nutrients and other raw materials; serves as a foundation for human construction efforts such as roads or buildings; and stores, filters, and purifies water. It also provides a habitat for millions of animals, such as moles, worms, and mice, and other organisms, from fungi to insects.

Because of soil's tremendous importance to our lives and the lives of other living creatures, it is crucial that we track what is in it. Farmers must be especially conscious of the amount of minerals in their soil, for example. They also have to track its texture or average temperature and its level of acidity (how much acid is in the soil). There are many ways to perform soil tests that

*Many farms and gardens work hard to maintain their "organic" labels by avoiding pesticides and soil additives, while letting nature do most of the work.*

analyze all of this information. Some are very low-tech and have been around for hundreds of years. For example, you can test soil's water **infiltration** rate by driving a tube into the ground, pouring in an amount of water, and measuring how much of the water has drained over a certain time period. More complicated tests are usually done in a lab by trained chemists.

The recent trend toward **organic** farming in many parts of the world has led to new considerations in soil testing. Organic farming depends on the natural release of nutrients already within the soil. To understand how these nutrients cycle, more frequent testing is necessary. Organic farming also uses nutrient-rich compost to aid growth. Since too many nutrients can damage water quality, tests must be done to see how many nutrients are released.

## Portable Testing

In some of the poorest regions of Africa, farmers lack the tools to adequately test their soil. This makes it difficult for them to maximize their food production. When University of Maryland soil scientist Ray Weil was working in Africa, he conceived of the idea of a portable soil testing kit that could help farmers diagnose their cropland. With researchers from Columbia University, he designed a kit that contains battery-operated instruments and other testing equipment. Trained agents use the kit to test soils out in the field. They send the results via cell phone to a central website. The site runs the calculations and provides information to the farmers on the amount of nutrients and organic matter in the soil.

One new development in soil testing is the use of synchrotron [SINK-roh-tron] technology. A synchrotron is a machine that accelerates particles, often electrons, to nearly the speed of light. As the electrons pass through different types of magnets, they create high-powered X-rays. The light from these X-rays is billions of times brighter than that of the sun. The machine can be used to examine tiny particles of matter, down to the atoms and molecules. Scientists **employ** this technology to study soil.

A Canadian study using synchrotron light looked at how different nitrogen fertilizers affected the chemistry of soil. This is important, since nitrogen fertilizers are often applied to enrich soils, but they can have long-lasting environmental effects. The

This massive machine is a synchrotron. As light is whirled throughout its thousands of feet of tubes, scientists can test how that light affects soil and other materials.

*Agricultural science is not just for the lab. Experts known as agronomists must head into the fields to see how their theories and studies play out in real life.*

scientists tested three main types of nitrogen fertilizers: synthetic, or man-made, fertilizers; animal manure; and crops like lentils and soybeans that can harness nitrogen directly from the air. The study showed that nitrogen is essential for old plant matter to break down completely into soil. In this the manure-based fertilizers were most effective.

### Energy From Oats

Next time you eat oatmeal, you might be helping to reduce overall carbon-dioxide emissions. When we burn coal alone, there is a high amount of these emissions. Environmental researchers in Iowa have found that burning oat hulls, the outer casings of oat seeds, along with coal cuts the amount of emissions by 40 percent. It also reduces the amount of hazardous particles and heavy metals such as copper and zinc that coal releases into the air. Oat hulls are an example of biomass, which is any plant-based energy source. Other examples of biomass include algae, cornstalks, and one of mankind's oldest forms of energy, firewood.

# Battling Disease

No matter how many times farmers test their soil, it may not be enough to keep away **infectious** plant diseases. Citrus greening disease is one example: caused by a strain of bacteria spread by tiny insects, it destroys citrus trees by turning their fruit green, hard, and inedible, and by damaging their roots. Infected trees die within a few years. It can have a devastating impact on the citrus industry, both in America and abroad.

In Florida, where oranges and other citrus are a $10.7 billion industry, the threat of citrus greening disease has been especially dangerous. Since 2007, the state has lost some 100,000 citrus trees and $3.6 billion in revenue due to the disease. Using the science of genetic engineering, where genes from one organism are used to modify another, researchers from the University of Florida recently developed a new citrus tree that resists greening. The researchers used a gene isolated from a tree from the mustard family. This gene helps the new trees defend themselves against bacteria. More work has to be done before the trees are available to farmers, such as transferring the gene to the many varieties of citrus grown in Florida. But at least growers can take heart in knowing that a cure for the **blight** is on the way.

## New Fuel Sources

Another thing scientists do to improve the quality of the environment is look for and test alternative fuel sources. Burning fossil fuels like coal, oil, and natural gas puts out high levels of carbon dioxide. Dependence on them has had a negative effect

*The bacteria known as citrus greening has turned this once-healthy lime into another piece of fruit for the trash. The disease is costing millions of dollars a year.*

on the environment, contributing to climate change, pollution, acid rain, and other problems. In their place, many scientists advocate the use of renewable resources such as geothermal, solar, wind, or water power. These "clean" fuels do not pollute to the degree that fossil fuels do. They can also be easily renewed with little risk.

▶ *This powder, which might become a new source of fuel, comes from the process known as methane cracking, which separates methane into its component parts.*

A new chemical procedure, however, might allow for the use of natural gas as an energy source without harmful carbon dioxide emissions. This new technique is called "methane cracking." Methane is the main component of natural gas. Instead of burning it directly, scientists have figured out how to split it into its base elements: carbon and hydrogen.

For their experiment, physicists designed a special reactor. Methane bubbles are inserted into the base of a tube of molten tin. The methane "cracks" when it rises to the surface and encounters the liquid metal, as the carbon separates out as a powder. The resulting hydrogen can then be used as a clean energy source in fuel cells or hydrogen-powered vehicles. The carbon is not wasted: It can be resold for use in making steel and other material production. In the coming years, physicists will continue to "scale up" their reactor, eventually making it large enough for industrial use.

## Creating Clean Water

While some scientists are developing new environmentally friendly methods of energy production, others are cleaning up the damage caused by old ones. For instance, Canadian researchers have developed a novel way to **decontaminate** the wastewater left over from oil production.

Alberta, Canada, is home to the third-largest oil reserve in the world. In 2014 alone, 2.3 million barrels were extracted from the site. The process of getting the oil out requires a lot of water. Much of this is reused, but a portion is not. This ends up in massive pools called tailing ponds. There are 30 square miles (77 sq km) of tailing ponds in Alberta alone. The danger is that they can spill over, causing soil erosion in nearby lands and endangering the health of wildlife and water systems.

To combat this problem, the researchers only use two things: sunlight and tiny particles (called nanoparticles) of titanium dioxide. When the light hits the particles, it causes a reaction, and the particles break down the bacteria, pollutants, and other organisms in the water. The best part is that the particles can be removed from the water afterward and reused over and over. Other environmentally safe methods of destroying the pollutants in tailing ponds have been tried in the past, including the use of algae, but this new method is by far the cheapest and most efficient. However, it has only been tested on small samples. The next step is making sure the particle-purified water is safe enough to be let out of the large tailing ponds.

It isn't only wastewater from tailing ponds that needs to be addressed: freshwater sources must be tended to in order to ensure good quality and steady supply. In Wisconsin, environmental scientists have studied how subtle shifts in the composition of a landscape can greatly benefit freshwater sources. As it is now, much of Wisconsin—and other states in the Midwest—is divided into sections of farmland, wetland, grassland, and man-made towns and cities. Altering the varieties and sizes of these sections, where possible, is a good way to improve water sources.

The reason behind this is that a landscape's layout greatly affects how nutrients pass between land and water. Agricultural areas tend to have excess nutrients from farming, which can run off and pollute nearby water sources. Natural barriers such as forests and prairies between farms and water sources can absorb these nutrients in a much healthier way. Environmental scientists are quick to point out that these kinds of changes do not have to be drastic, since it can be difficult to reorder whole segments of land. Instead, they advise small changes such as increasing the amount of wetlands and making small reductions to the amount of cropland.

*The huge ponds in this image are the tailing ponds of nearby mining operations. How these ponds are cleaned and how they work with the environment is in the news.*

This may look just like the edge of a parking lot—and it is—but it's also a scientifically designed urban rain garden intended to maximize water use in drought conditions.

Other strategies include planting rain gardens, which are depressions or holes filled with deep-rooted plants and grasses. Rainwater gathers pollutants as it runs over streets, driveways, parking lots, and other man-made landscapes. Typically, this runoff goes into storm drains, which empty into rivers, lakes, and bays. Rain gardens planted in urban areas absorb this runoff and prevent it from entering into freshwater systems. The gardens filter the runoff naturally so it can be used by surrounding plant life.

# Text-Dependent Questions

1. What are some ways that soil is essential to life on Earth?

2. What is citrus greening disease, and why is it so dangerous?

3. What are the two main things used to clean tailing ponds in environmentally safe ways?

# Research Project

Research home soil-testing methods, such as the Mason jar soil test for soil structure or the various tests for soil pH using household ingredients. Run these tests on soils from your yard or neighborhood. Using your results, research ways to improve soil quality as necessary—for example, increasing drainage if there's too much clay or adding ground limestone to raise pH. Write a brief "soil profile" summarizing your findings and recommendations.

What is environmental science?

This coffee grower in Africa might be able to take advantage of new technologies that use satellites in space combined with cell phones to help make his farm more profitable.

# TECHNOLOGY AND
# Environment and Sustainability

## Words to Understand

**cataclysmic**   relating to an event that is especially violent or disastrous

**genome**   an organism's entire set of DNA, including all its genetic material

**materials science**   a branch of science involving the research and development of new materials for construction or manufacturing, involving metals, plastics, and others

**sequestered**   in environmental studies, relates to the amount of carbon stored through natural or artificial means as a way to limit the effects of climate change

**socioeconomic**   concerning the relationship between social (where a person lives) and economic (what types of jobs are available) factors

In the previous chapter, we saw how cell phone technology is helping farmers in remote parts of Africa connect to soil-testing services that improve their agriculture. Physical scientists have teamed up with social scientists to launch another cell-phone-based technology that can help predict the possibility of famine and malnutrition in the world's most impoverished areas. The system analyzes data on weather and soil conditions alongside **socioeconomic** information about a particular place.

First, soil data is gathered by satellite. This is a unique technology in and of itself. Radar on the satellite scans the Earth's surface with microwaves, while another instrument determines how much radiation the Earth is emitting. The variations in the signals supply information about the temperature and moisture of the soil. Satellites repeat the process every two to three days. Captured data is plotted on maps so that farmers and scientists alike can see which places are most vulnerable to drought.

Meanwhile, in disaster-stricken or other vulnerable areas, researchers go out into the field to gather notes on the availability of food and the health of the farmland. They also examine political or social conditions (such as violence or terrorism) that threaten people's lives. The researchers input their findings into a smartphone app, which assigns them a GPS coordinate. The app then creates a map of all the shared information that is compared alongside the satellite-derived soil moisture map. Taken together, these two maps form a more complete picture of where humanitarian aid is needed most.

## Measuring Methane

Another new technology that is helping with high-level environmental mapping is a camera that measures the amount of methane in the air. Methane is the second most emitted greenhouse gas due to human activity. It comes primarily from the raising of livestock and from leaks in natural gas energy systems, though wetlands and other natural sources also produce it. Methane in the air traps the sun's heat. This warms the air and contributes heavily to climate change.

## SMAP and Soil Data

In addition to tracking the possibility of drought, soil data gathered by satellite is also helpful in determining weather patterns and potential for floods. Soil moisture influences the weather when it evaporates; it leaves the surface of the Earth drier and, therefore, cooler. By knowing the amount of water in the soil before a rainstorm, scientists can tell which areas are wetter and more likely to flood.

Satellites like the Soil Moisture Active Passive (SMAP) satellite, launched in January 2015, also show how resources are exchanged between land and air through the soil. By assessing moisture levels, we can gain a better understanding of how water, carbon, and other energy sources cycle through the earth. To collect all this vital information, the SMAP satellite is equipped with a 20-foot (6.1 m) rotating mesh antenna—the largest ever used in space.

*The SMAP satellite, shown here in a NASA artist's view, aims at large areas of Earth and gathers soil, water, and agricultural information for use by scientists.*

The new camera was designed by researchers in Sweden. Its development required knowledge from many different fields, including astronomy, engineering, and environmental science. The 77-pound (34.9 kg) instrument is known as a hyperspectral infrared camera, which means it can measure the amount of electromagnetic radiation in the air as well as the amount of heat. Researchers program the camera to detect the type of radiation that methane absorbs. The resulting image shows the methane particles separately from other gases in the atmosphere. So far, scientists have used the camera in methane-heavy environments on land: sewage deposits, farms with livestock, and lakes. In the coming years, they're hoping to get it airborne so they can begin tracking methane levels on a wider scale.

## Oil Spill Cleanup

Like greenhouse gases, oil spills have become an all-too-common threat to our environment. Sometimes this happens naturally, as when a deposit of oil or gas trapped beneath the earth leaks to the surface. More often than not, however, these spills are the result of human activity—for instance, a pipeline bursts or a tanker or drilling rig malfunctions. The results can be **cataclysmic**, with widespread damage to plant, animal, and human life. Spills can take years to clean up, prolonging the effects and costing millions of dollars in the process.

The ultimate solution for oil spills is to prevent them from occurring in the first place. Until this happens, emerging technologies in **materials science** have led to a new way of reducing their effects. Like a sponge on steroids, a high-tech material called a boron nitride nanosheet can absorb more than 30 times its weight in oil. These sheets could drastically cut down the time it takes to clean up after a spill.

In its first phase of development, the sheet was simply a powder known as "white graphite." The powder was able to absorb oil, but there was no way to retrieve it if it was used on water. Researchers formed the powder into sheets only nanometers thick—or thin, rather, since a nanometer is only one billionth of a meter! These "nanosheets" have tiny pore-like holes. The design allows them to increase their available surface area so they can soak up huge amounts of oil.

## Tech and Trees

New technologies in the field of environmental science are not just for specialists. Programs like the US Forest Service's Tree Carbon Calculator are available online for anyone to use. Though the software was originally developed for the state of California, it has expanded to cover 16 climate zones across the whole United States. When the user enters information about a particular tree's size, age, species, and/or location, the program returns a whole range of information about the tree's environmental impact. It

**Refugio Oil Spill**

A recent survey revealed that the U.S. oil and gas industry averaged 20 spills per day of various sizes, amounting to more than 26 million gallons (98 million l) of oil, gas, and related substances. One of the biggest spills in recent years was near Refugio State Beach in Santa Barbara County, California, in spring 2015. An underground pipeline two feet (61 cm) in diameter burst just north of the beach. The pipeline, which was 28 years old, did not have an automatic shutoff valve. By the time operators shut it down, more than 140,000 gallons (530,000 l) of crude oil spilled along the coast, damaging several miles of beaches and harming wildlife. At least 21,000 gallons (79,500 l) of oil reached the ocean, creating a slick that stretched more than nine miles (14 km) before a frantic disaster operation stopped its spread. Cost of cleanup: nearly $100 million.

## i(Seed)Pod

The United States Department of Agriculture (USDA) sponsors a collection of online tools designed specifically for "urban forestry"—that is, the use of trees to beautify cities and make city-dwellers' lives more healthful. The tools are collectively known as i-Tree and have many different applications. Each helps urban planners, local officials, and community residents find the most effective ways to plant trees in their cities and towns. A few of the applications include:

· *i-Hydro* lets users see how trees would impact water quality, flow of streams, and flood prevention

· *i-Tree Design* compares and contrasts the benefits of different planting locations, including how trees can save energy and improve air quality

· *i-Tree Streets* analyzes the costs of tree-planting projects in urban areas, as well as how they can help save money

· *i-Tree Vue* helps urban foresters see how many trees are currently planted in different areas, and to test out the best places to add new trees

For a complete overview of the i-Tree software, see the Forest Service-sponsored site at **http://www.itreetools.org/.**

tells the user how much carbon the tree has **sequestered** over the past year and throughout its life, the amount of energy-supplying biomass the tree would produce if cut down, and the energy it saves by helping to heat or cool nearby buildings.

A more recent version of the Tree Carbon Calculator, ecoSmart, has some additional features. With Google Maps, users can mark their property and lay out different landscape designs. The software computes the environmental benefits of each one, both now and into the future.

When a tree is cut down, all the carbon it has stored up to that point remains within the wood for several decades. The program PRESTO (PRoduct EStimation Tool Online) lets timber companies see how much carbon these harvested wood products (like lumber or paper) are holding onto. The Carbon OnLine Estimator (COLE) is good for businesses and governments, since it analyzes forest carbon amounts across large areas like counties and states.

*This may look like a huge forest of beautiful trees, but it's also a massive oxygen generator. Trees literally help keep us alive by producing oxygen.*

## Helping the Air With Plants

One way to cut down on greenhouse gas emissions is to limit the use of synthetic fertilizers. They are man-made fertilizers used to increase the amount of nitrogen in soils, which is good for growing crops. Before synthetic fertilizers were invented, farmers relied on clover and bean crops like lentils to enrich their soil with nitrogen. These crops are able to take nitrogen out of the air. With the help of bacteria that grows in their roots called *rhizobia*, they are able to convert it for use by the soil.

*Red clover is often used by farmers because the plant has a unique characteristic of adding useful nitrogen back into the soil as it grows and feeds.*

Red clover is very efficient at this process. It is also an excellent feed for livestock since it is naturally high in protein. The problem is that red clover is not very hardy. It grows for two or three seasons at most, and grazing livestock can significantly damage it. To tackle these problems, scientists are using the latest in genetic engineering technology, in which individual pieces of DNA are reordered and reassembled to create a new **genome**. Scientists took specific genetic material from different strands of red clover to produce a genome that will make the plant stronger. It will now be able to endure grazing and ward off disease. Breeders use the genome to reproduce the plant on a larger scale. The more resilient crop of red clover will be better for farmers and make a more eco-friendly fertilizer.

**Text-Dependent Questions**

1. How does methane in the air contribute to climate change?

2. What are some causes of oil spills? What are some of their effects?

3. Why are natural fertilizers like red clover better for the environment than synthetic fertilizers?

 **Research Project**

Find and download one of the online tree carbon calculators or forestry management tools profiled in this chapter. Experiment with them by finding how much carbon a tree from your climate zone is sequestering. Write a brief report summarizing your findings, as well as any recommendations you might have to make the program better.

Renewable vs. fossil fuels

Next time you reach for a nice, cool, clean glass of drinking water, think about the many miles it has traveled to reach you and the many machines, people, and processes that brought it there.

# ENGINEERING AND
# Environment and Sustainability

## Words to Understand

**biomes**   types of ecological communities; specific geographic areas, including all the plants and animals that naturally thrive there

**desalination**   the process of removing salt from a substance such as seawater or soil

**fiber-optic**   a type of thin, translucent wire that transmits information via pulses of light

**hydrologists**   people who study the composition, distribution, and movement of water on the Earth

**ingenuity**   inventiveness; the skill of creating a solution to a complex problem

**irrigate**   to supply water to an area of land

**tsunami**   a massive ocean wave caused by an earthquake or volcanic eruption

Regardless of who you are or where you live, you need fresh drinking water. Like air or food, hydration—the body's ability to take in and use water—is essential to human life, and the process of supplying it to people is a task that involves many different environmental science professionals. **Hydrologists** look for available sources; chemists develop tests to reveal possible contamination; and engineers design, install, and operate the vast systems that deliver water from sources like reservoirs or wells into our homes.

The light-shaded areas on the shores of this reservoir in California show just how much the water level has fallen as that state battles a long drought.

In the past several years, the **ingenuity** of these professionals has been tested as different parts of the world battle water shortages known as drought. Droughts can be caused by human activities as well as natural changes in weather cycles. Rising global temperatures lead to faster evaporation of rainfall and snowmelt, which can result in drought. Heat also dries out soil and makes it more difficult for plants to retain water. High ocean temperatures that prevent rain clouds from reaching shores, overuse of the water supply, and dams or irrigation systems that limit water flow are other factors that increase the likelihood of drought.

Environmental scientists say that the best way to decrease drought is to change our water-use habits, making more efficient home appliances and finding ways to recycle and reuse water. While these are excellent long-term solutions, a rapidly growing world population has increased the demand for water at an alarming rate.

*The flip side to drought is unusual flooding. These rescue workers fanned out to help people in central England when heavy rains made rivers overflow their banks.*

## Water Recycling

Like desalination, water recycling is seen as one of the best ways to combat drought. In this process, water used by households and businesses is collected, purified, and released back into the environment; it can then be used by plants, animals, or humans. This so-called toilet-to-tap method may sound unhygienic at first, but the procedure is based on ways that lakes and streams purify themselves naturally.

First, incoming water is filtered through screens to remove any large debris. It is then sent to a tank where a whirlpool-like motion separates out dirt particles and other sediment. Air is added to the water along with bacteria that eat up any contaminants. The bacteria is left to settle to the bottom of the tank, where it is either reused to clean more water or else converted into fertilizer. Finally, the water is blasted with ultraviolet light that sanitizes any remaining bacteria. Within 24 hours, it is returned to local watersheds.

In fact, it's predicted that the worldwide need for water will grow by 55 percent by the year 2050.

# Taking Salt From Water

To meet this demand, environmental engineers have stepped up production of **desalination** plants in various parts of the world. These plants remove salts and other minerals from seawater, which can then be used for drinking, farming, or industry.

The concept of desalination is an ancient one. Greek and Roman cultures from thousands of years ago would use special clay filters or would boil water to separate out the salt. The large-scale systems of today use a process called reverse osmosis. Salt water is forced at high pressure through membranes with small, pore-like holes. The membranes hold back the salt, letting only water molecules pass through. The fresh water that comes out the other side is then redirected to homes and businesses.

There are three times as many desalination plants around the world today as there were in 2000. More than 16,000 of them are in operation, with especially large operations in Saudi Arabia and Australia. A new plant in Carlsbad, California, is expected to filter 54 million gallons (204 million l) of drinkable water per day. This is a crucial addition to California's water supply, as severe drought has plagued

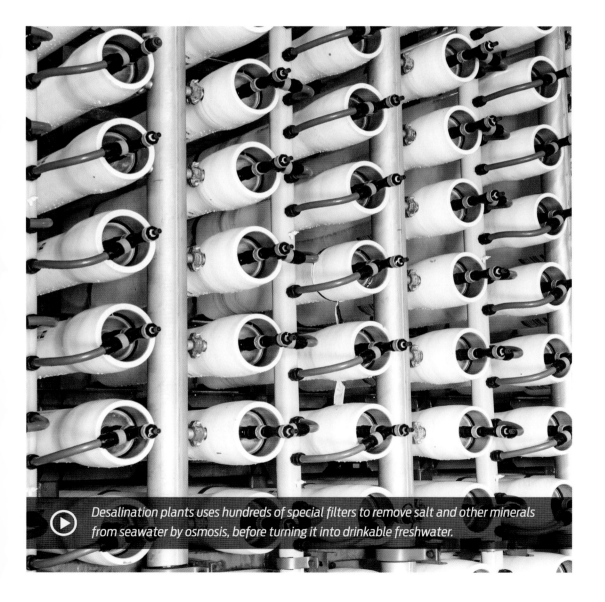

*Desalination plants uses hundreds of special filters to remove salt and other minerals from seawater by osmosis, before turning it into drinkable freshwater.*

the state for years. The system itself was a huge undertaking for engineers, requiring 18 house-sized water tanks and 2,000 fiberglass tubes. There are also extra pumps to serve as backups in case something fails.

## Alternative Power Sources

Drought is far from the only environmental danger currently facing humanity. We have seen how reliance on fossil fuel energy sources such as coal, oil, and natural gas has affected our

*Nuclear energy remains a viable alternative energy source. However, it is also controversial, as its long-term effects and possible dangers are debated.*

The 2011 earthquake and tsunami that hit Japan came close to destroying an onshore nuclear plant. The disaster was terrible, but could have been even worse.

environment. Such sources produce gases that trap heat and contribute to an overall rise in the Earth's temperature. Nuclear power, an alternative to fossil fuels, does not release gases but is dangerous in other ways. It produces radioactive waste, which is very hazardous to humans and other forms of life and can take millions of years to decay.

In 2011, a massive earthquake off the coast of Japan caused a **tsunami** to strike the Fukushima nuclear power plant. Several of

*This model shows the location of Japan's Fukushima nuclear plant. You can see how a massive tidal surge, caused by the earthquake, could overwhelm the facility.*

the plant's nuclear reactors—the parts that generate power—were damaged by the water, and large amounts of radioactive material were released into the environment. More than 100,000 people had to be evacuated from the area to avoid being exposed. Under pressure from the Japanese public, the event spurred companies to begin exploring other sources of energy. Among them was solar, the use of the sun to create power. The difficulty with solar is that it requires a lot of land. Solar cells, the silicon panels that are used to capture sunlight and convert it into electricity, may spread across hundreds of acres. That is a problem in a small country like Japan. So environmental engineers came up with a solution: build the solar power plants on water.

In 2013, Japan opened its largest solar plant to date, a 314-acre (127 ha) operation on Kagoshima Bay. The 290,000 solar panels are waterproof and generate enough electricity for 22,000 homes. In late 2014, construction began on two "solar islands" that will float on the surfaces of reservoirs. Besides saving space, the panels will actually work better on the water, since they run more efficiently when cool. Norwegian engineers recently designed a solar island that would join 4,200 panels to float atop the ocean, proving that the trend of offshore solar plants continues to grow.

*A floating island of energy? Solar power needs solar cells, and those cells need room to spread out. In land-starved Japan, this offshore solar island fills the bill.*

# Better Sanitation

The simplicity, low cost, and abundance of solar power make it a good alternative for future energy needs. One unlikely place it is being used by engineers is in the design of new sanitation facilities in India, China, and Africa. Solar-powered toilets can help stop the spread of disease in places that lack adequate sanitation.

## Glowing and Growing

Taking FluxNet's tower design to (literally) new heights, scientists at the California Institute of Technology have been experimenting with collecting information on plant activity—from space. When plants are performing photosynthesis—the process of turning sunlight and carbon dioxide into food and releasing oxygen—they put out near-infrared light that is invisible to the human eye. However, it can be captured by instruments that measure light intensity called spectrometers. Spectrometers are already installed on satellites orbiting the Earth, such as NASA's Orbiting Carbon Observatory-2. By studying the amount of light detected by the spectrometer, scientists can analyze the overall productivity of plants around the world.

One version of the solar-powered toilet focuses the energy of the sun with eight specially shaped mirrors. The heat is transferred to a quartz rod, which is then transferred to bundles of **fiber-optic** cables. The cables heat a "reaction chamber" to 600°F (315°C). This is hot enough to sterilize waste and turn it into biochar, a form of charcoal that can be used to improve soil quality. Another version uses solar energy to power an electrochemical reactor. The reactor separates waste into fertilizer and hydrogen. The hydrogen can be reused as fuel to power the toilet on days when there isn't enough sun. In addition, the toilet has a solar-powered pump that treats and recycles wastewater. This can be used to flush the toilet or even be sent out to **irrigate** crops.

Solar-powered toilets like these might be able to improve sanitation in areas where running water is rare by using the power of the sun to keep them clean.

Engineers are now at work designing sensors that monitor a toilet's condition. If a part of the toilet breaks down, a text message would be sent via cell phone to a local technician. The technology would help speed up maintenance, since many of the toilets will be installed in remote parts of the world.

Solar power is not the only technology engineers are harnessing to improve sanitation systems. Biodigester toilets use huge tanks to separate waste into gases and manure. The gases can be turned into an energy source—to light stoves or produce electricity, for instance—while the nutrient-rich manure can be recycled as fertilizer for farms. Another toilet uses the principle of composting. This is when bacteria in decaying organic matter like plants, grass clippings, or food scraps turns it naturally into fertilizer. For this to happen, the organic matter needs the right amount of moisture and air. Indoor composting toilets have a small drum to collect waste; the drum spins to provide the necessary oxygen. Every three months it is emptied, and the compost can be put to use.

*Sometimes, simple is better. This basic composting toilet (put in some sawdust after you go to speed things along) can convert waste into a soil additive.*

This is one of 650 FluxNet towers scattered around the world. They constantly monitor a wide range of weather and atmospheric conditions.

# Tracking Change

To track the effects of all these alternative energy projects on the environment, scientists turn to a data-gathering network known as FluxNet. There are more than 650 FluxNet towers across the globe. The towers are equipped with hydrometers, which measure the amount of water vapor in the air; infrared gas sensors, which analyze the amounts of carbon dioxide and other gases; and anemometers, which are devices that gauge wind velocity. Together, these tools measure the exchanges of energy between the earth and the atmosphere. What is unique about FluxNet is that most towers update data every 30 to 60 minutes. This gives ecologists a sense of the small changes that occur in the atmosphere throughout the day.

*This closeup view of a FluxNet device shows the wind-speed and direction monitors (cross arm) plus the guy wires that hold the device steady.*

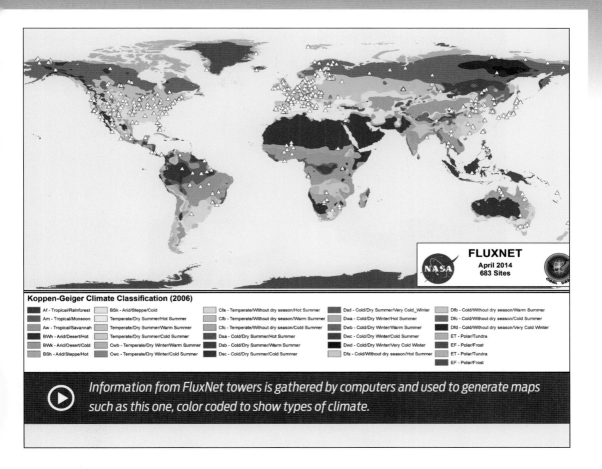

Koppen-Geiger Climate Classification (2006)

FLUXNET
April 2014
683 Sites

Information from FluxNet towers is gathered by computers and used to generate maps such as this one, color coded to show types of climate.

Engineers who construct the towers have specific things to consider when selecting a site. They need to make sure the plant cover in the area is consistent and that the landscape is relatively level. Otherwise, information on the amounts of carbon and other gases in the air would be inconsistent. Engineers must also take care to place sensors in safe places on the towers. This means knowing the average wind speed, tower height and height of surrounding trees, and how often the sensors will capture data. Sensors placed on very tall towers have to be mounted on long rods away from the towers themselves. That's because tall towers

FluxNet engineers will go wherever the weather is, even if that takes them to far-off and icy places such as this one.

can be unsteady, and their added motion can make wind-speed readings inaccurate.

The individual FluxNet towers are linked to a central database, so scientists can compare information from different places and times. That allows them to study global energy patterns as well as the impact of different environments. There are towers on five continents, in **biomes** including grassland, tundra, tropical forest, wetlands, and others.

# Text-Dependent Questions

1. How do desalination plants help meet humanity's water needs?

2. What are some ways that new sanitation facilities are using solar power?

3. Why is it important for some FluxNet sensors to be mounted away from tall towers?

 # Research Project

Research ways that people in your community, such as home-builders, merchants, farmers, or local leaders, are using engineering solutions to help preserve the environment. Examples might include "rails-to-trails" programs that turn old railroad beds into environmentally friendly bike trails, or "passive house" construction techniques that incorporate solar energy, green roofs, and heat recovery systems.

India's sanitation battle

*The work of environmental scientists starts in the field. The data and samples that they gather are turned into statistics and studies that look for ways to improve the world in which we live.*

# MATH AND
# Environment and Sustainability

## Words to Understand

**algorithm**   a process or set of operations used to solve a problem or discover new information

**elongating**   extending; making longer

**polygons**   closed figures bounded by a number of line segments

**quantify**   to measure the amount of something in numbers

**seismologist**   a person who studies earthquakes

**troves**   vast collections of something

**A**s we have seen throughout this book, the changing mix of the earth's temperature, atmosphere, soil, and other natural elements has given environmental scientists much to work on. In addressing the challenges we face, it is important for scientists to **quantify** these changes. For example, only by knowing how many degrees temperatures are rising in certain areas can we begin to see patterns and start to solve problems. That is why math is such a crucial part of environmental study.

Take the **algorithm** scientists developed to fight the effects of water pollution. The algorithm evaluates three different ways a water pollutant behaves: diffusion, when it moves from areas of high concentration to low concentration; convection, when it is pushed along by natural forces, such as waves or currents; and reaction, when it reacts to other elements in the water or stops moving on its own. By plugging these factors into the algorithm, scientists can determine each pollutant's origin as well as how quickly it moves within a body of water. This information will help avert environmental disasters by identifying "hot spots" where pollutants are leaking in time to treat them.

This view of Los Angeles from the 1980s shows how bad the air used to be there. A special monitoring system called AQI continues to tell people about their air quality.

# Measuring Good Air

Similarly, a mathematical process is used in determining air-pollution levels of cities worldwide. The Air Quality Index (AQI) is the number that scientists use to represent how many pollutants are in the air in a certain place at a specific time. The U.S. Environmental Protection Agency developed the index. It measures six different types of pollutants: sulfur dioxide, nitrogen dioxide, carbon monoxide, ozone (a gas that is a main component of smog), particulate matter (small particles of pollutants such as metal, acids, or dust), and fine particulate matter (like particulate matter, only smaller).

An AQI reading is taken every 24 hours. However, in Singapore, where pollution levels can be abnormally high, a separate reading of fine particulate matter is taken every three hours. The AQI is rated on a scale of zero to 500, with zero being the safest and anything above 300 being the most dangerous. An AQI above 100 is considered "unhealthy," and certain groups of people (such as children or the elderly) may show signs of illness. Anything above 300 is classified as "hazardous," and area residents are advised to stay indoors.

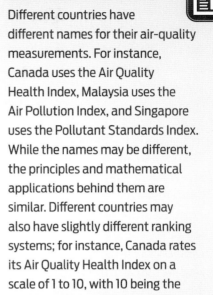

## Quality Control

Different countries have different names for their air-quality measurements. For instance, Canada uses the Air Quality Health Index, Malaysia uses the Air Pollution Index, and Singapore uses the Pollutant Standards Index. While the names may be different, the principles and mathematical applications behind them are similar. Different countries may also have slightly different ranking systems; for instance, Canada rates its Air Quality Health Index on a scale of 1 to 10, with 10 being the most severe. Europe's Common Air Quality Index generates three different values: an hourly index, a daily index, and an annual index. The air quality of nearly 100 European cities is used to gather these figures.

# The Two-Degree Threshold

In December 2015, leaders from nations around the world gathered in Paris for the United Nations Climate Change Conference. One of the major goals of the conference was to agree to limit the global average temperature to no more than 2°C above pre-industrial levels (i.e., the time before the Industrial Revolution in the 18th century). In the end, more than 190 countries signed on to the agreement, one of the most important international moves in battling climate change. The agreement, however, is just the start. Every country has to do its part; the proof won't be known for decades.

The math behind the number in the agreement was a combination of scientific intuition, data analysis, and what changes countries can realistically make to their energy use. Worldwide temperatures have already risen by 1°C—and, with the natural changes in the climate, are expected to rise an additional 0.5°C. This makes the 2°C goal very difficult to reach, especially since the world is only beginning to address the problem now. One multinational panel ran calculations on 400 different energy-reduction plans to see which had the best chance of keeping the Earth below the 2°C threshold. The problem with many of these plans is that they depend on technology that isn't readily available yet. Some officials see the 2°C limit as more of a "guideline," while others recognize a need for dramatic changes now if we hope to sustain ourselves as a planet.

*French president François Hollande, commission president Lauren Fabius, and UN Secretary-General Ban Ki Moon applaud the 2015 climate agreement.*

# Decoding Earthquakes

Algorithms are not only used to measure pollutants, but also to identify large-scale environmental activities such as earthquakes. A new computerized algorithm called FAST (Fingerprint and Similarity Thresholding) is able to scan vast amounts of data to identify small earthquakes known as microquakes that would otherwise go undetected. The algorithm's main developer likens it to Shazam, a popular app that can identify entire songs based on short sections.

The FAST process uses whole **troves** of information collected from seismic stations, underground chambers that measure the Earth's ground motion. That motion is represented by waves. FAST "cuts" the long strands of recorded wave activity into short sections of a few seconds each. Sections with similar wave patterns are grouped together and tracked to the time when they occurred. Scientists can then "search" ground motion data for specific types of earthquakes, or compare new wave patterns with old ones. Since FAST doesn't have to run through every pattern stored in the database, but instead zeroes in on matching patterns, the searches are up to 3,000 times faster than previous techniques. By finding and analyzing microquakes through FAST, **seismologists** are better able to predict where and when larger—and more dangerous—earthquakes will occur.

# Math and Maps

Above ground, environmental scientists must also sift through many sets of data in order to assess landscapes, identify problems, and come up with solutions. To do this they use geographic information systems (GIS), a type of computer mapping program that captures, saves, analyzes, and displays multiple layers of information about a specific place. All kinds of information—numerical and otherwise—can be included on a GIS map: the population density of a given area, for instance, can be presented alongside data on nearby farms or forests. This helps environmental scientists make necessary comparisons and establish relationships between various elements of a place.

Several mathematical concepts are used in GIS mapping. Existing paper maps must be digitized using geometry. The digitizer traces the basic geometric components of the map, such as **polygons** or lines, in order to represent it on a computer. Coordinate geometry, a type of geometry that locates points in space with labels called coordinates, is used to match information about a specific place with its correct location on the map. Maps of three-dimensional surfaces must be altered to fit in two dimensions, such as on a piece of paper or a computer screen. Different maps have different alterations, **elongating** some areas while shrinking others. GIS applications use geometry to synthesize these many maps into a single representation. To depict the steepness and direction of terrain (technically referred to as its "slope" and "aspect"), GIS operators employ linear algebra and trigonometry.

Once GIS maps are compiled and standardized, they can run calculations to help users find specific information. For example, a "clip tool" is a way of searching for a piece of data within a selected area, such as the amount of forested land within a city's limits. A "buffer" is an area of a defined distance around a fixed point—say, a one-mile (1.6 km) radius around a geological feature. By setting these sorts of numerical parameters, users can better focus their searches. This is especially helpful since GIS systems have so many "data layers," or overlapping maps, each with a different focus.

The uses of GIS are growing every day. Land surveyors can use GIS to evaluate construction sites, examine water sources and soil quality, and access government records about a particular

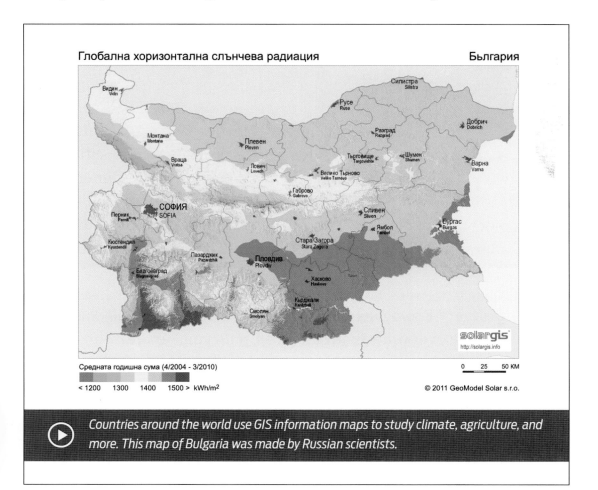

Глобална хоризонтална слънчева радиация    България

Средната годишна сума (4/2004 - 3/2010)

< 1200    1300    1400    1500 >  kWh/m²

0    25    50 KM

© 2011 GeoModel Solar s.r.o.

solargis
http://solargis.info

*Countries around the world use GIS information maps to study climate, agriculture, and more. This map of Bulgaria was made by Russian scientists.*

A seaside flood in Greece brought out a host of volunteers that had to use boats to help survivors. In the future, forecasting floods will save lives.

property. Ecologists can analyze forest resources and changes in climate over time. In urban areas, policymakers can consult GIS programs to see which neighborhoods are most vulnerable to flooding or other natural disasters. They can also find relationships between social factors (like income or education level) and geographical ones (such as where public transport or parkland is most accessible). They can then use this information to make decisions that will best serve their communities.

# Planning for Floods

Mathematics in the environmental sciences isn't all advanced geometry and algorithms. Nor is it always tied to physical terrain. In some cases it is addressing environmentally related problems, such as ensuring equal access to disaster insurance or coming up with strategies to reduce carbon emissions.

With the rise in climate change, the risk of flooding has increased in many coastal areas of the United States. A new report from the U.S. Congress has advised the Federal Emergency Management Agency (FEMA) to redesign flood insurance plans to be more affordable. This would involve recalculating what homeowners can realistically pay for flood insurance, then coming up with ways of providing assistance.

# Calculating Carbon

The tourism industry is a huge part of international commerce, creating one in 11 jobs worldwide. Yet it is also one of the biggest sources of pollution and carbon emissions. Air travel, ground transport, hotels, and other travel-related businesses account for almost five percent of the world's total carbon output. One way to reduce overall emissions is through carbon offsets—an amount of money someone pays, almost like a tax, that goes to help fund carbon-reducing projects in other parts of the world. Researchers have calculated that a fee of just $11 per tourist per trip could go a long way in funding carbon-reduction efforts. It would help ensure that future generations enjoy the same destinations we travel to see today.

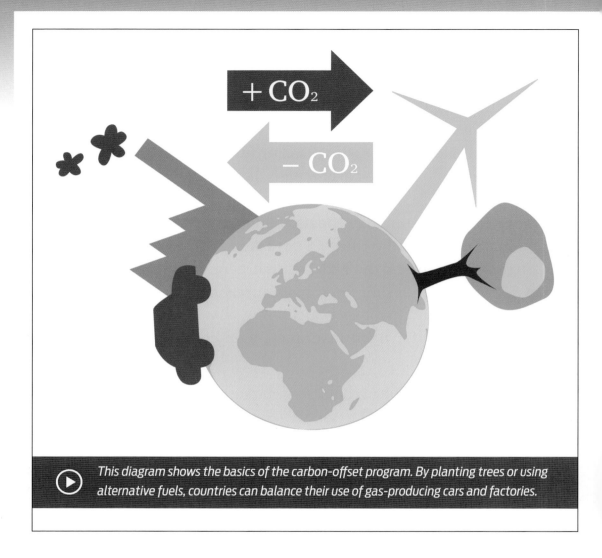

This diagram shows the basics of the carbon-offset program. By planting trees or using alternative fuels, countries can balance their use of gas-producing cars and factories.

The first step to protecting our environment is understanding it, so science and math play a huge part. The next step is finding tools and techniques to make changes that make Earth more sustainable. That's where technology and engineering come in. Together, the fields of STEM are helping make sure that the world's fields, oceans, and animals will be around for a long time.

# Text-Dependent Questions

1. What types of pollutants does the Air Quality Index measure?

2. How is seismic wave activity organized within the FAST system?

3. What are some ways that geometry is used to create geographic information systems?

 # Research Project

Using the website Airnow.gov, research air quality levels for different cities in your area of the country. How do these levels compare with each other and with other American and international cities? How do current conditions match up with projected forecasts? Do you notice any correlation between a city's location and its air quality level? Write a brief report summarizing your findings, being sure to include details on specific pollutants if available.

Check out this carbon footprint calculator; how did you do?

# Find Out More

## Books

Maczulak, Anne E. *Environmental Engineering: Designing a Sustainable Future (Green Technology)*. New York: Facts on File, 2009.
How scientists are approaching environmental issues through technology.

Royston, Angela. *The Race to Survive Climate Change (World in Crisis)*. New York: Rosen Publishing Group, 2015.
Part of a series that explores how scientists and societies are seeking new ways to address world problems.

## Websites

Phys.org is a continually updated site featuring news on science topics from around the world. Everything from astronomy and space to nanotechnology to Earth and environmental science is covered.
*phys.org/*

The online magazine *Gizmag* covers all things tech: new inventions, profiles of industry leaders, and the latest technologies in fields as diverse as architecture, sports, and travel.
*www.gizmag.com/*

*Science News*, the official magazine for the Society for Science & the Public, is available in both print and online formats. The website features science-related stories from around the world, as well as a blog with shorter pieces on related topics.
*www.sciencenews.org/*

The well-established *Smithsonian* magazine, the official publication of the Smithsonian Institution, covers innovations in science, art, culture, and other fields, fostering a sense of discovery and creativity.
*www.smithsonianmag.com*

# Series Glossary of Key Terms

**capacity**   the amount of a substance that an object can hold or transport

**consumption**   the act of using a product, such as electricity

**electrodes**   a material, often metal, that carries electrical current into or out of a nonmetallic substance

**evaporate**   to change from a liquid to a gas

**fossil fuels**   a fuel in the earth that formed long ago from dead plants and animals

**inorganic**   describing materials that do not contain the element carbon

**intermittently**   not happening in a regular or reliable way

**ion**   an atom or molecule containing an uneven number of electrons and protons, giving a substance either a positive or negative charge

**microorganism**   a tiny living creature visible only under a microscope

**nuclear**   referring to the nucleus, or center, of an atom, or the energy that can be produced by splitting or joining together atoms

**organic**   describing materials or life forms that contain the element carbon; all living things on Earth are organic

**piston**   part of an engine that moves up and down in a tube; its motion causes other parts to move

**prototype**   the first model of a device used for testing; it serves as design for future models or a finished product

**radiation**   a form of energy found in nature that, in large quantities, can be harmful to living things

**reactor**   a device used to carry out a controlled process that creates nuclear energy

**sustainable**   able to be used without being completely used up, such as sunlight as an energy source

**turbines**   an engine with large blades that turn as liquids or gases pass over them

**utility**   a company chosen by a local government to provide an essential product, such as electricity

# Index

# Credits

# About the Author

**Michael Centore** is a writer and editor. He has helped produce many titles for a variety of publishers, including memoirs, cookbooks, and educational materials, among others. He has authored several previous volumes for Mason Crest, including titles in the Major Nations in a Global World and North American Natural Resources series. His essays have appeared in the *Los Angeles Review of Books*, *Killing the Buddha*, *Mockingbird*, and other print- and web-based publications. He lives in Connecticut.